No longer property of Anythin
No longer property of Anythink Libra

D0899026

LEARN

Hindi

WORDS

clock
घड़ी
(gharii)

teddy bear
टेडी बेयर
(tedi-beyar)

doll
गुड़िया
(guriyaa)

pillow
तकिया
(takiyaa)

blanket
कम्बल
(kambal)

bed
बिस्तर
(bistar)

BY M. J. YORK • ILLUSTRATED BY KATHLEEN PETELINSEK

The Child's World®
childsworld.com

Published by The Child's World®
1980 Lookout Drive • Mankato, MN 56003-1705
800-599-READ • www.childsworld.com

Acknowledgments
Translator: Mithilesh Mishra, PhD, Senior Lecturer and
Director, Hindi-Urdu and South Asian Languages, Department
of Linguistics and Global Studies, University of Illinois at
Urbana Champaign

Copyright © 2020 by The Child's World®
All rights reserved. No part of this book may be reproduced or
utilized in any form or by any means without written permission
from the publisher.

ISBN 9781503835849
LCCN 2019944695

Printed in the United States of America

ABOUT THE AUTHOR

M. J. York is a children's author and editor living in Minnesota. She loves learning about different people and places.

ABOUT THE ILLUSTRATOR

Kathleen Petelinsek loves to draw and paint. She also loves to travel to exotic countries where people speak foreign languages. She lives in Minnesota with her husband, two dogs, and a fluffy cat.

CONTENTS

Introduction to Hindi

One of India's most-spoken languages is Hindi. It is common in northern India. More than 600 million people around the world speak it. Many Hindi speakers live in Nepal, South Africa, and Singapore, too.

Hindi has roots in Sanskrit, an ancient language of India. It is similar to Urdu, a language of Pakistan. It has influences from Persian and English, too. Hindi has many dialects. The version used in schools and governments is called modern standard Hindi.

Hindi is written in the Devanagari script. Symbols in this script are linked together, similar to cursive. Unlike in English, each symbol always represents one unique sound. There are several ways to write Hindi using Roman letters. This book uses the Hunterian system. Letters mostly are pronounced as in English.

Notes on Hunterian Pronunciation

aa   as in f**a**r, p**a**lm, or f**a**ther

ii   as in m**ea**t, ch**ea**p, or s**ea**t

uu   as in c**oo**l or f**oo**l

N   indicates the vowel before it is nasalized, with air let out through the nose

Vowels

अ   a as in **a**bout
आ   as in f**a**ther
इ ई   i as in s**i**n
इ ई   i as in mach**i**ne
उ   u as in p**u**ll

ऊ   u as in r**u**de
ए   e as in b**e**t
ऐ   ai sounds like s**i**te
ओ   o as in b**o**ne
औ   au sounds like n**o**w

Consonants

क	k	त	t (said with teeth closed)	ल	l
ख	kh	थ	th (said with teeth closed)	व	v
ग	g	द	d (said with teeth closed)	श	sh (said with the mid tongue)
घ	gh	ध	dh (said with teeth closed)	ष	sh (said with the tip of the tongue)
ङ	ng as in si**ng**	न	n (said with teeth closed)	स	s
च	ch	प	p	ह	h
छ	chh as in pit**ch h**ook	फ	ph as in u**ph**ill	क़	q
ज	j	ब	b	ग़	gh
झ	jh	भ	bh	ख़	kh (hissed)
ञ	ny	म	m	ज़	z
ट	t	य	y	फ़	f
ठ	th	र	r as in ra**re**	ढ़	rh
ड	d			ड़	r
ढ	dh				
ण	n				

My Home
मेरा घर
(meraa ghar)

window
खिड़की
(khir-kii)

bathroom
बाथरूम
(bath-rum)

lamp
लैम्प
(laimp)

bedroom
बेडरूम
(bed-rum)

television
टेलीविजन
(teli-vijza)

kitchen
किचेन
(kichen)

cat
बिल्ली
(billii)

living room
ड्रॉइंग रूम
(drawing-rum)

sofa
सोफ़ा
(sofaa)

chair
कुर्सी
(kursii)

table
मेज़
(mez)

In the Morning
सुबह में
(subah meN)

clock
घड़ी
(gharii)

teddy bear
टेडी बेयर
(tedi-beyar)

doll
गुड़िया
(guriyaa)

pillow
तकिया
(takiyaa)

bed
बिस्तर
(bistar)

blanket
कम्बल
(kambal)

9

At the Park
पार्क में
(paark meN)

Let's play!
चलो, खेलें।
(chalo kheleN!)

sky
आकाश
(aakaash)

friend
दोस्त
(dost)

soccer ball
फुटबॉल
(phut-baul)

bird
चिड़िया
(chiriyaa)

MORE USEFUL WORDS

game
खेल
(khel)

sports
खेल-कूद
(khel-kuud)

13

Around Town
शहर में
(shahar meN)

airplane
हवाई.जहाज
(hawaai jahaaj)

office
ऑफ़िस
(aufis)

building
इमारत
(imaarat)

bus
बस
(bas)

2100
OFFICE
BUILDING

CITY BUS

MORE USEFUL WORDS

truck
ट्रक
(trak)

train
ट्रेन
(tren)

stop
रुकिये
(rukiye)

go
जाइये
(jaa-i-ye)

15

My Birthday Party
मेरे जन्म-दिन की पार्टी
(mere janm-din kii paartii)

grandmother (paternal)
दादी
(daadii)

I am six years old.
मेरी उम्र छह साल है।
(merii umr chhah saal hai.)

grandfather (paternal)
दादा
(daadaa)

sister
बहन
(bahan)

brother
भाई
(bhaai)

cake
केक
(kek)

MORE USEFUL WORDS

one एक *(ek)*	eleven ग्यारह *(gyaarah)*
two दो *(do)*	twelve बारह *(baaarah)*
three तीन *(tiin)*	thirteen तेरह *(terah)*
four चार *(chaar)*	fourteen चौदह *(chaudah)*
five पाँच *(paaNch)*	fifteen पंद्रह *(pan-drah)*
six छह *(chah)*	sixteen सोलह *(solah)*
seven सात *(saat)*	seventeen सत्रह *(satrah)*
eight आठ *(atah)*	eighteen अठारह *(athaarah)*
nine नौ *(nau)*	nineteen उन्नीस *(unniis)*
ten दस *(das)*	twenty बीस *(biis)*

19

Time for Dinner
डिनर का समयें
(dinar ka samay)

At Night
रात में
(raat meN)

Good night!
शुभ रात्रि!
(shubh raatri!)

MORE USEFUL WORDS

Today is Friday.
आज शुक्रवार है
(aaj shukr-waar hai.)

Yesterday was Thursday.
कल गुरुवार था।
(kal guru-waar thaa.)

Tomorrow is Saturday.
कल शनिवार है।
(kal shani-waar hai.)

bathtub
बाथटब
(baath-tab)

I am tired! (male)
मैं थका हूँ!
(maiN thakaa huuN!)

22

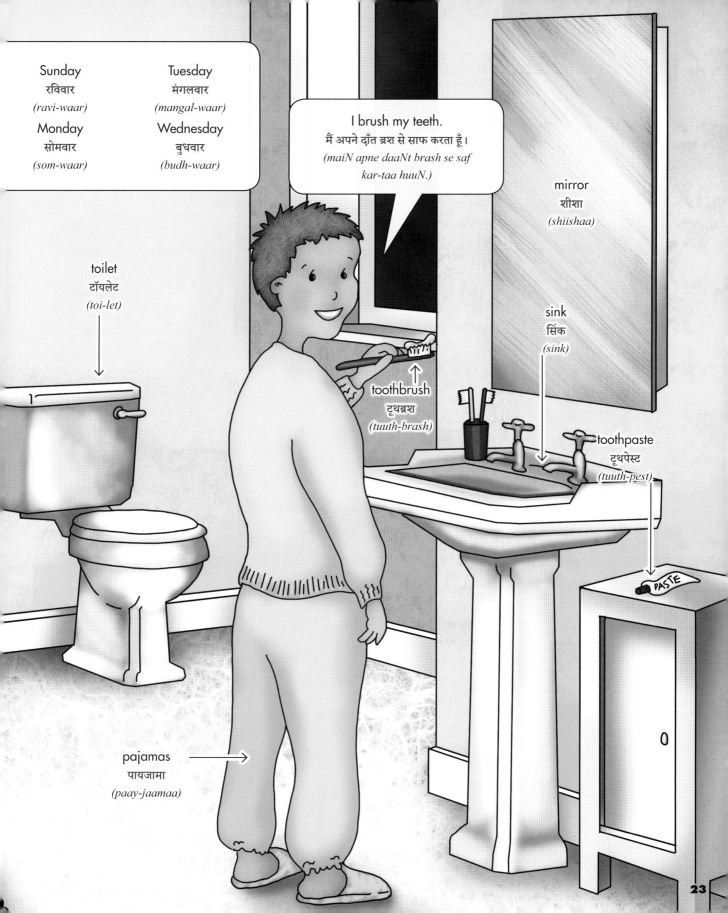

23

MORE USEFUL WORDS

Yes
हाँ
(haaN)

No
नहीं
(nahiiN)

ten
दस
(das)

twenty
बीस
(biis)

thirty
तीस
(tiis)

forty
चालीस
(chaaliis)

fifty
पचास
(pachaas)

sixty
साठ
(saath)

seventy
सत्तर
(sattar)

eighty
अस्सी
(assii)

ninety
सन्बे
(nabbe)

one hundred
सौ
(sau)

January
जनवरी
(janwarii)

February
फरवरी
(pharwarii)

March
मार्च
(maarch)

April
अप्रैल
(aprail)

May
मई
(mai)

June
जून
(juun)

July
जुलाई
(julaai)

August
अगस्त
(agast)

September
सितम्बर
(sitambar)

October
अक्टूबर
(oaktuubar)

November
नवंबर
(nawambar)

December
दिसंबर
(disambar)

winter
सर्दी का मौसम
(sardii kaa mausam)

spring
बसंत काल
(basant kaal)

summer
गर्मी का मौसम
(garmii kaa mausam)

fall
पतझड़ का मौसम
(patjarh kaa mausam)

good-bye!
नमस्ते !
(namaste!)